Vocal Selections from

Finian's Rainbow

Music by **Burton Lane**

Lyrics by **E.Y. Harburg**

Alfred Music Publishing Co., Inc.
16320 Roscoe Blvd., Suite 100
P.O. Box 10003
Van Nuys, CA 91410-0003
alfred.com

ISBN-10: 0-7390-6401-0
ISBN-13: 978-0-7390-6401-6

"One of the mightiest
musical clicks in history"
—Walter Winchell

LEE SABINSON and WILLIAM R. KATZELL

present

FINIAN'S RAINBOW

A Completely Captivating Musical

Book by
E. Y. HARBURG and FRED SAIDY

Lyrics by
E. Y. HARBURG

Music by
BURTON LANE

Directed by
BRETAIGNE WINDUST

Scenery and Lighting by
JO MIELZINER

Dances and Musical Numbers by
MICHAEL KIDD

Costumes by
ELEANOR GOLDSMITH

Orchestrations by
ROBERT RUSSELL BENNET and DON WALKER

Vocal arrangements by LYN MURRAY

"Inspired smash musical" —NEWSWEEK

Original show poster for the
1947 Broadway production.

Contents

The Show

A masterful combination of wit, topical satire, sentiment, and soaring musicality, *Finian's Rainbow* was the smash hit of the 1947 Broadway season. In fact, there are few musicals that can boast as many hits that became standards, including "How Are Things in Glocca Morra?" "Look to the Rainbow," and "Old Devil Moon." *Finian's Rainbow* was unusual in that it was not based on any previously published play or book, but instead sprang from the fertile mind of lyricist E. Y. "Yip" Harburg (1896–1981).

In 1946, Harburg, an unabashed supporter of leftist causes, became enraged by the actions of two politicians from Mississippi: Senator Theodore Bilbo and U.S. Representative John Rankin. Bilbo (1877–1947) was an unapologetic racist, a member of the Ku Klux Klan, and a supporter of segregation. Rankin

Photofest

David Wayne (Og) and Ella Logan (Sharon), in a scene from the original 1947 Broadway production of *Finian's Rainbow*.

The original Broadway cast album featured Ella Logan on the cover.

(1882–1960) used offensive epithets against Jews and African Americans on the floor of the House of Representatives and once called the KKK an "American Institution." It was Harburg's notion to write a show with a bigoted politician, patterned after Bilbo and Rankin, who is magically transformed into a Negro, just to see how he would feel to be treated like one. While reading James Stephens's novel *The Crock of Gold*, Harburg got the inspiration to mask his idea with a whimsical, magical Irish fantasy. Harburg took his fanciful idea to composer Burton Lane (1912–1997), who agreed to write the melodies.

Although not as prolific as other theater composers, Burton Lane wrote superlative scores for a variety of motion picture musicals and Broadway shows. In addition to Harburg, his lyricist collaborators included Ira Gershwin, Frank Loesser, and Alan Jay Lerner. His score for *Finian's Rainbow* features a stunning variety of musical styles, including charming Irish-tinged melodies, satirical gospel numbers, and comic songs that showcased his natural wit and sense of humor. Michael Feinstein once said that Lane was as great a composer as George Gershwin or Irving Berlin; high-powered company indeed. Although *Finian's Rainbow* became his most celebrated Broadway score, he did not write another for nearly 20 years.

Of course, since this was Broadway, there had to be a romantic angle, so Harburg and co-librettist Fred Saidy (1907–1982) fashioned a plot about two Irish immigrants: Finian and his daughter, Sharon, who arrive in Missitucky's Rainbow Valley with a crock of gold Finian stole from a leprechaun named Og. Because America's gold reserve is buried at Fort Knox, it is Finian's belief that the stolen gold will multiply if he buries it nearby. When the two arrive in the valley, they learn that Missitucky's racist senator, Billboard Rawkins, seeks to take the land away from the sharecroppers and immigrants who live on it. (In his rant, Rawkins delivers one of the great laugh lines in the annals of Broadway: "My whole family's been havin' trouble with immigrants ever since we *came* to this country!")

Sharon falls in love with Woody, a young labor organizer (modeled after folk singer Woody Guthrie) who needs to pay taxes on the land he owns in the valley. Finian provides Woody with the money he needs, and, in turn, Woody gives Finian some land where he can bury his gold. Senator Rawkins, however, seizes the land after he accuses Woody of allowing Negroes to live on the property. An angry Sharon makes a wish that the Senator be transformed into a black man to see how the other half lives, and her wish is magically granted. Rawkins, now black, joins a black gospel quartet. Og, realizing he is slowly becoming mortal, falls in love with Woody's mute sister Susan. The show ends happily as a now-reformed Rawkins is turned white again, Sharon and Woody marry, and Og and Susan become betrothed. As the show closes, Finian moves on, still pursuing his rainbow.

The original Broadway cast of *Finian's Rainbow* starred Ella Logan as Sharon, David Wayne as the leprechaun Og (for which he won a Tony), Albert Sharpe as Finian, Donald Richards as Woody, and Robert Pitkin as Senator Rawkins. The show was a huge hit, playing for 725 performances. A popular film version was made in 1968, starring Fred Astaire as Finian and Petula Clark as Sharon. The songs from *Finian's Rainbow,* a beguiling combination of Irish ballads, American gospel, and rousing production numbers, constitute one of the best-loved scores in musical theater history.

The Songs

"How Are Things in Glocca Morra?" sung by the winsome Irish immigrant, Sharon, became the most popular theater song of the 1947 season. It has a wistful Irish-tinged melody with lyrics that summon up the image of a magical land, mentioning a litany of evocative Irish place names such as Killybegs, Kilkerry, and Kildare. Hit versions of the song in 1947 include recordings by Buddy Clark, Martha Tilton, and Dick Haymes.

"Look to the Rainbow," which is also sung by Sharon, sums up Yip Harburg's optimistic philosophy and the inspirational theme of the show. Harburg's poetic lyrics are some of his most expansive and passionate. The young Harburg and his family had been decimated by the stock market crash of 1929, but he kept his dreams alive by becoming a songwriter, thanks to a long-standing friendship with Ira Gershwin. "Look to the Rainbow" shows that fate runs in cycles: despair is followed by triumph if one only looks to the rainbow. The lyrics feel similar to those in another Harburg song, from the magical production *The Wizard of Oz,* for which he wrote "Follow the Yellow Brick Road" to describe another pathway to an idealistic goal. (That show featured another inspirational song about a rainbow, sung by Judy Garland.)

The power of the moon is suggested in a duet sung by Sharon and Woody, "Old Devil Moon," which has challenged singers ever since with its difficult melodic line and intricate harmonic shifts. Thanks to successful recordings by Frank Sinatra and Mel Tormé, "Old Devil Moon" has since rivaled "How Are Things in Glocca Morra?" as the show's most enduring song, having become a jazz standard performed by Carmen McRae, Sarah Vaughan, and other jazz stars.

"Something Sort of Grandish" is a duet sung by Sharon and Og, the mischievous leprechaun who is experiencing love for the first time. For this song, Harburg fashioned a frivolous lyric full of words with invented suffixes, forced rhymes (such as "fowl or fish" with "Eisenhowsish"), and a puckishly whimsical melody.

Infatuated with each other, Woody and Sharon sing "If This Isn't Love," a vigorously amorous list song loaded with giddy metaphors and more forced rhymes (like "William Tell / Adora-bel") that express the breezy silliness some feel when in love.

"Necessity" is Yip Harburg's wry take on labor and religion in society. The song begins like a spiritual, but then becomes an irreverent commentary on how practical matters interfere with the joys of living. It is sung by the black sharecroppers in Rainbow Valley.

"That Great Come-and-Get-It Day" is a rousing song celebrating economic freedom that closes Act I. Sung by the citizens of Rainbow Valley in the spirit of a spiritual jubilee, the residents express their delight when they receive news that they have had unlimited

Fred Astaire (Finian) and Petula Clark (Sharon) starred in the 1968 motion picture version of *Finian's Rainbow.*

credit extended to them by the mail-order house of Shears and Robust (a take-off on Sears, Roebuck & Co.).

After being transformed into a black man, Senator Rawkins joins the Passion Pilgrim Gospeleers quartet in a satirical song about the population explosion. "The Begat" features a pseudo-spiritual melody by Burton Lane with lyrics by Harburg that are reminiscent of those in Cole Porter's list song "Let's Do It (Let's Fall in Love)."

Stephen Sondheim once called "When I'm Not Near the Girl I Love" to be "the greatest eleven o'clock song in the annals of the American musical." David Wayne's performance as Og made him a star, mostly due to this song, in which Og shows his fickle nature by neatly transferring his affections from Sharon to Susan. Harburg's playful lyrics cleverly twist meanings with brilliant palindromic turns in nearly every phrase.

Cary Ginell

Popular Music Editor
Alfred Music Publishing Co., Inc.

HOW ARE THINGS IN GLOCCA MORRA?

Words by
E.Y. HARBURG

Music by
BURTON LANE

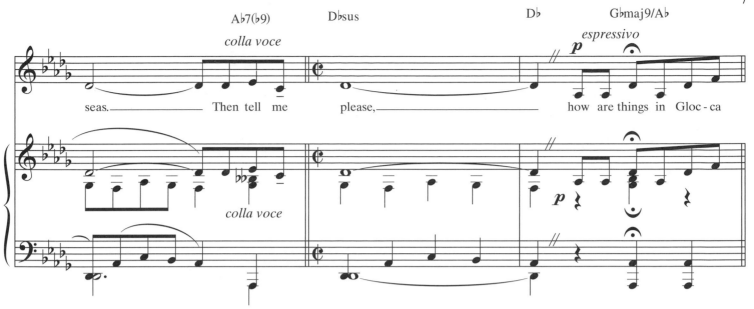

Lento espressivo (♩ = 56)

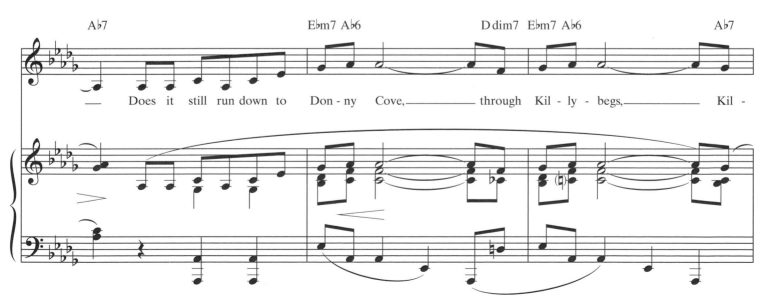

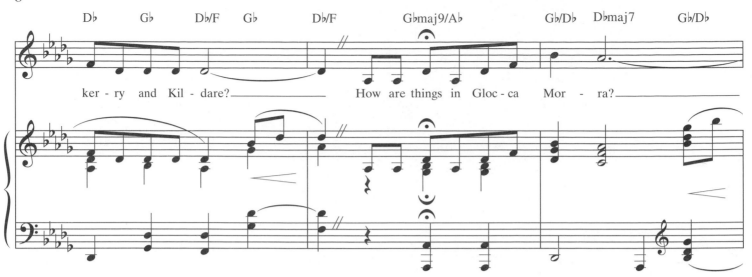

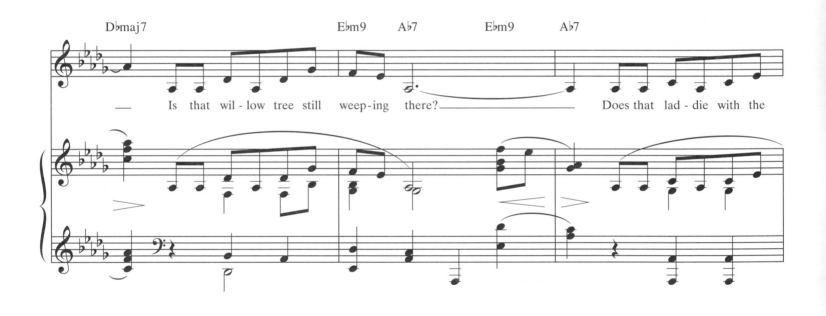

LOOK TO THE RAINBOW

Words by
E.Y. HARBURG

Music by
BURTON LANE

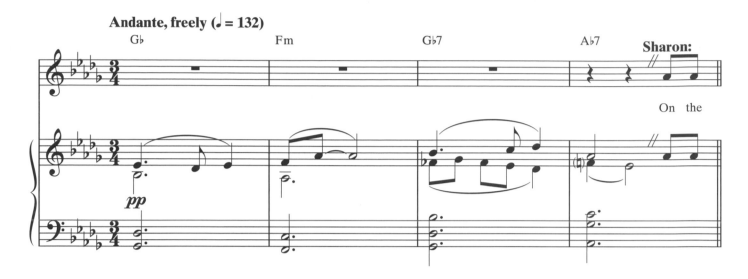

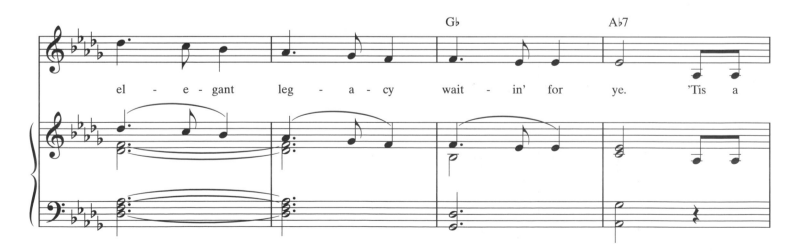

Look to the Rainbow - 5 - 1
33623

OLD DEVIL MOON

Words by
E.Y. HARBURG

Music by
BURTON LANE

Old Devil Moon - 4 - 1
33623

Old Devil Moon - 4 - 3
33623

SOMETHING SORT OF GRANDISH

Words by
E.Y. HARBURG

Music by
BURTON LANE

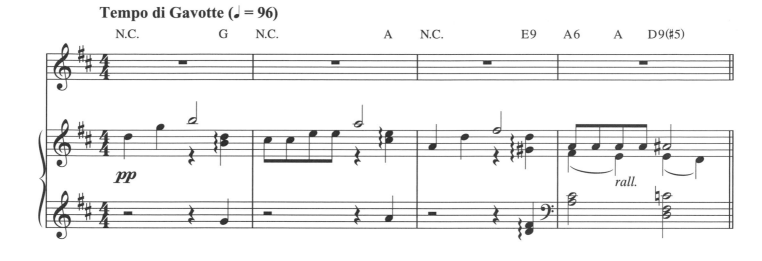

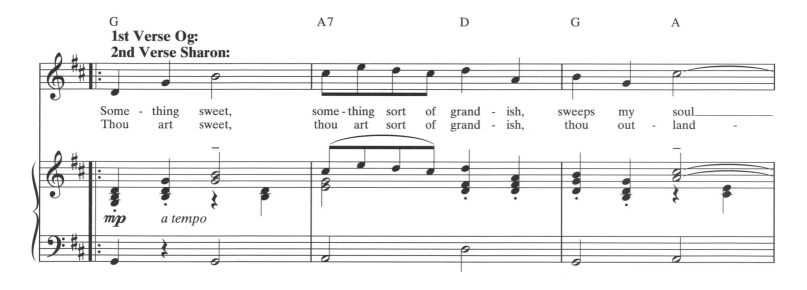

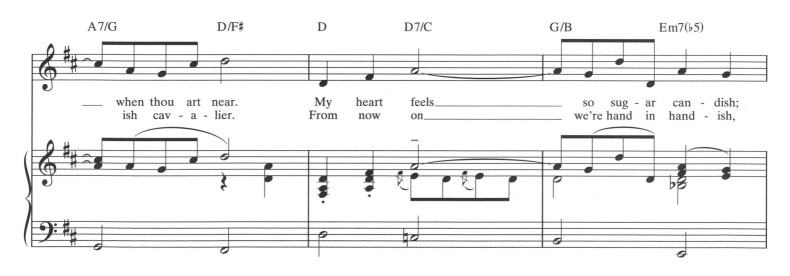

Something Sort of Grandish - 3 - 1
33623

IF THIS ISN'T LOVE

Words by
E.Y. HARBURG

Music by
BURTON LANE

Refrain: (**Joyously**)

NECESSITY

Words by
E.Y. HARBURG

Music by
BURTON LANE

Recitative (very slowly)

What is the curse that makes the u-ni-verse so all be-

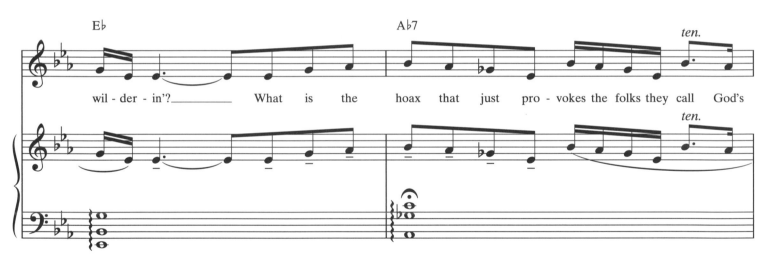

wil-der-in'?_____ What is the hoax that just pro-vokes the folks they call God's

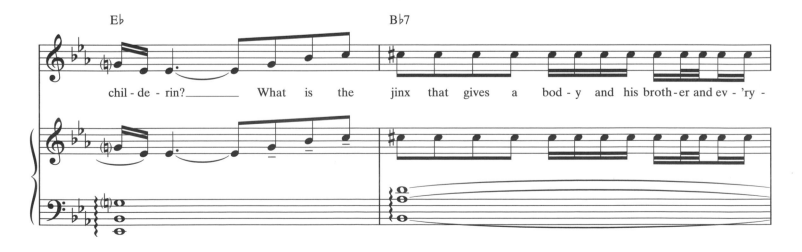

chil-de-rin?_____ What is the jinx that gives a bod-y and his broth-er and ev-'ry-

Necessity - 5 - 1
33623

THAT GREAT COME-AND-GET-IT DAY

Words by
E.Y. HARBURG

Music by
BURTON LANE

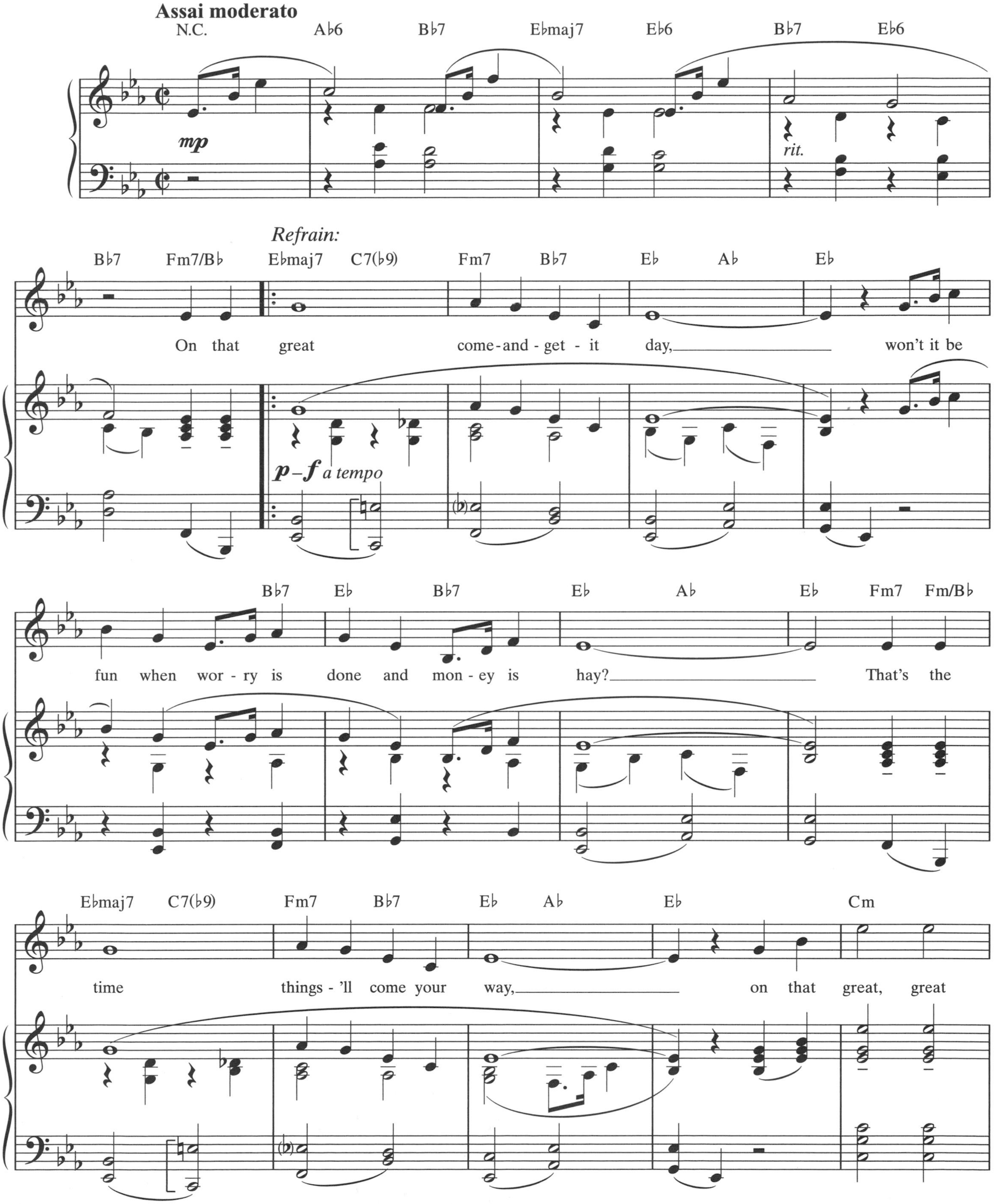

Assai moderato
N.C. A♭6 B♭7 E♭maj7 E♭6 B♭7 E♭6
mp
rit.
Refrain:
B♭7 Fm7/B♭ E♭maj7 C7(♭9) Fm7 B♭7 E♭ A♭ E♭
On that great come-and-get-it day, won't it be
p–f a tempo
B♭7 E♭ B♭7 E♭ A♭ E♭ Fm7 Fm/B♭
fun when wor-ry is done and mon-ey is hay? That's the
E♭maj7 C7(♭9) Fm7 B♭7 E♭ A♭ E♭ Cm
time things-'ll come your way, on that great, great

THE BEGAT

Words by
E.Y. HARBURG

Music by
BURTON LANE

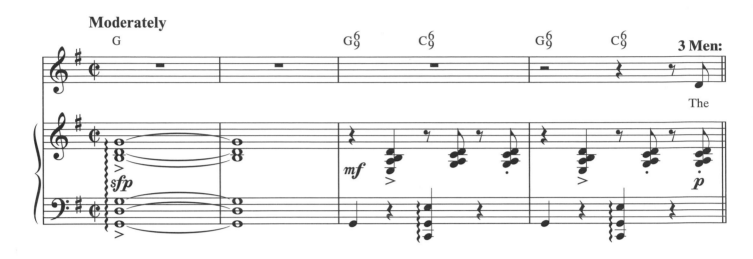

The Begat - 10 - 1
33623

WHEN I'M NOT NEAR THE GIRL I LOVE

Words by
E.Y. HARBURG

Music by
BURTON LANE

When I'm Not Near the Girl I Love - 4 - 1
33623